HOME
DECORATING
Walls

HOME
DECORATING
Walls

Techniques and ideas for the walls of your home – a complete step-by-step guide

MIKE LAWRENCE

HERMES HOUSE

This edition first published in 1997 by Hermes House

© Anness Publishing Limited

Hermes House is an imprint of
Anness Publishing Limited
Hermes House
88–89 Blackfriars Road
London SE1 8HA

ISBN 1 901 289 15 X

A CIP catalogue record for this book
is available from the British Library

Publisher: Joanna Lorenz
Project Editor: Judith Simons
Assistant Editor: Daniel King
Designer: Michael Morey
Photographer: John Freeman
Illustrator: Andrew Green

Printed and bound in Hong Kong

Previously published as part of a larger compendium,
The Complete Book of DIY and Decorating.

PUBLISHER'S NOTE
The author and publishers have made every effort to ensure that all instructions contained
within this book are accurate and safe, and cannot accept liability for any resulting injury, damage
or loss to persons or property however it may arise. If in any doubt as to the correct procedure
to follow for any home improvements task, seek professional advice.

PICTURE CREDITS
The publishers would like to thank the following companies for permission to reproduce the following pictures in this book:
t = top; b = bottom; c = centre; l = left; r = right; Crown Paints, front jacket main, back jacket tl tr, back flap b, page 39 br,
Cuprinol Ltd, page 13 bl br; Dulux, front jacket tl cr, back jacket cl, pages 10/11, 11 br, 12 tl, 13 t; Forbes-CP (Fablon) Ltd,
front flap, pages 2 tl br, 3; Forbo-Kingfisher Ltd, front jacket bl, pages 2 bc, 6, 37 t; Harlequin Wallcoverings Ltd,
front jacket tr, page 2 tc; Harrison Drape, page 2 bl.

1 3 5 7 9 10 8 6 4 2

C O N T E N T S

INTRODUCTION   6

PAINTING   8

TYPES OF PAINT, VARNISH
AND STAIN   10

PAINTING TOOLS AND EQUIPMENT   14

PATCHING WALL AND
CEILING DAMAGE   16

PREPARING SURFACES FOR PAINTING   18

STRIPPING PAINT   20

USING A PAINTBRUSH   22

USING PAINT ROLLERS AND PADS   24

PAINTING WALLS AND CEILINGS   26

SPECIAL PAINT EFFECTS   28

PAPERHANGING   34

TYPES OF WALL COVERING   36

PAPERHANGING TOOLS
AND EQUIPMENT   40

PREPARING FOR PAPERHANGING   42

STRIPPING OLD WALL COVERINGS   44

PREPARING SURFACES FOR COVERING   46

HANGING THE FIRST LENGTHS   48

PAPERHANGING AROUND CORNERS   50

PAPERHANGING AROUND DOORS
AND WINDOWS   52

PAPERING STAIRWELLS   54

PAPERING CEILINGS   56

OTHER PAPERHANGING TECHNIQUES   58

PUTTING UP FRIEZES AND BORDERS   60

REPAIRING WALL COVERINGS   62

Index   64

INTRODUCTION

This practical and inspirational new book helps you to make decisions about the most fundamental part of your indoor environment – the walls. While individual features can have a more immediate impact, it is the shade, texture and pattern of the walls that lend a room its overall atmosphere and influence choices of soft furnishing and interior accessories.

Painting remains the most popular way to embellish one's wall space, but its apparent simplicity can be misleading, so the first section of the book stresses the need to be familiar with materials and equipment and the importance of careful preparation, as well as giving useful hints on creating more ambitious paint effects, including stencilling, stippling and sponging.

On the other hand, applying wall coverings is far less complicated and taxing than is sometimes thought. Once again, preparation and the right equipment are paramount – the second section shows you how to tackle straightforward paperhanging tasks, awkward corners and shapes and more elaborate wall covering projects.

Illustrated throughout with step-by-step photography and explanatory diagrams, this book is an invaluable guide to producing individual, stunning walls with ease and at little cost.

OPPOSITE
With an ever-increasing range of materials to choose from,
you can mix and match different designs
to produce wonderful wall effects.

PAINTING

Painting walls, woodwork and other surfaces is, so all the surveys reveal, by far the most popular do-it-yourself job. Modern paints and improvements in the design and manufacture of decorating tools have certainly made the task less arduous than it was in the days of traditional oil-bound paints and distemper, and have also made it easier for the amateur decorator to get professional-looking results.

One major shift in paint technology is the trend away from using solvent-based varnishes and paints for wood, towards water-based products which do not give off harmful vapours as they dry. Water-based finishes are not as durable as solvent-based ones, but are no longer as far behind them in performance terms as they once were, and they have other advantages such as faster drying times, virtually no smell and easier cleaning of

brushes, rollers and pads. It is therefore likely that their use in the home will become much more widespread.

No amount of clever technology can eliminate the need for proper preparation of the surfaces to be decorated, even though this part of the job is far less enjoyable and often more time-consuming than the actual painting. In many cases it involves little more than washing the surface down, but sometimes more thorough preparation will be called for.

This chapter describes the various types of paint, varnish and stain on the market; which to use where; how to prepare surfaces for redecoration; how to apply the new finish – especially to the more awkward surfaces such as windows and panelled doors – and how to create a range of special paint effects that can be a dramatic and inexpensive alternative to wall coverings.

OPPOSITE
Paint offers a huge palette of colours, and
complementary and contrasting shades can
create the subtlest and most restful of colour
schemes. It is the easiest finish to change too
when a room needs a new look.

TYPES OF PAINT, VARNISH AND STAIN

Paint works by forming a film on the surface to which it is applied. This film has to do three things: it must hide the surface underneath; it must protect it; and it must stay put. All paint has three main ingredients: pigment, binder and carrier. The *pigment* gives the film its colour and hiding power. The *binder* binds the pigment particles together into a continuous film as the paint dries, and also bonds the film to the surface beneath. In traditional paint this was a natural material such as linseed oil in oil paints, or glue size in distemper; but modern paints use synthetic resins such as alkyd, acrylic, vinyl and polyurethane. The third ingredient, the *carrier*, makes the paint flow smoothly as it is applied, and evaporates as the paint dries.

The ratio of pigment to binder in a paint affects the finish it has when it dries; the higher the pigment content, the duller the finish. By adjusting this ratio, paint manufacturers can produce paints that dry to a flat *matt* finish; to a silky sheen, *eggshell*; or to a high *gloss*. The choice depends on personal preference, tempered by the condition of the surface: high-gloss finishes highlight any imperfections, while matt finishes tend to disguise them.

Paint types

The paint types used in the home have different carriers. Water-based paint has the pigment and binder suspended in water as tiny droplets. It is an emulsion, like milk, and is usually called *emulsion* paint. (In the USA it is

ABOVE The yellow water-based paint chosen for the walls of this kitchen creates a basically warm colour scheme that is off-set by the gloss paint in cool colours selected for the woodwork. Solvent-based (oil) paint is ideal for surfaces which need washing down regularly.

LEFT There is nothing like a hint of strong contrast to bring a neutral colour scheme to life, as the bright red bedposts and picture rail do so dramatically here. Paints specially formulated for steamy locations should be used in en-suite bathrooms.

RIGHT Blues and greys are cool, fresh colours that particularly suit a well-lit children's room. The brightly painted ladder provides the perfect contrast. Painted surfaces need to be able to withstand some rough treatment in these locations.

Paint systems

A single coat of paint is too thin to form a durable paint film. To provide adequate cover and performance there must be a paint system consisting of several coats. What these are depends on the type of paint used, and on the surface being painted.

The first coat is a *sealer*, which is used where necessary to seal in things such as the natural resin in wood, or to prevent the paint from soaking into a porous surface.

The second is a *primer*, which provides a good key for the paint film to stick to. On metal surfaces, this also stops the metal corroding or oxidizing. A primer can also act as a sealer.

The third is the *undercoat*, which builds up the film to form a flexible,

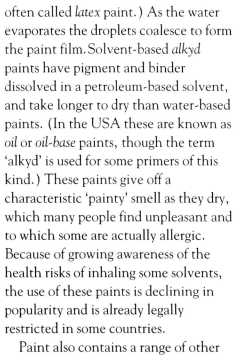

often called *latex* paint.) As the water evaporates the droplets coalesce to form the paint film. Solvent-based *alkyd* paints have pigment and binder dissolved in a petroleum-based solvent, and take longer to dry than water-based paints. (In the USA these are known as *oil* or *oil-base* paints, though the term 'alkyd' is used for some primers of this kind.) These paints give off a characteristic 'painty' smell as they dry, which many people find unpleasant and to which some are actually allergic. Because of growing awareness of the health risks of inhaling some solvents, the use of these paints is declining in popularity and is already legally restricted in some countries.

Paint also contains a range of other additives to improve its performance. The most notable is one that makes the paint *thixotropic* or non-drip, allowing more paint to be loaded onto the brush and a thicker paint film to be applied; one coat is often sufficient.

ABOVE A palette of yellow shades adds up to an irresistibly welcoming colour scheme for a baby's nursery.

LEFT Paint is not only for walls, ceilings and woodwork; it can also help to enhance the crisp lines of ornamental plasterwork.

BELOW Plain painted walls can be given a personal touch with hand-painted embellishments. Decorators with unsteady hands can use stencils instead.

ABOVE Sponging a second colour over a complementary base coat creates a soft broken-colour effect.

ABOVE Rag-rolling is another broken-colour effect that can look especially attractive when applied in stripes over the base colour.

non-absorbent base of uniform colour close to that of the fourth and final layer, the *top coat*, which gives the actual finish and colour.

On walls, for which water-based paint is generally used, the system consists simply of two or three coats of the same paint unless there is a need for a sealer or primer to cure a fault in the surface such as dustiness, high alkalinity or excessive porosity. The first coat is a *mist* coat of thinned paint. A primer is also used if walls are being painted with solvent-based paints.

On woodwork, the first step is to apply a liquid called *knotting* (shellac) to any knots to prevent resin from bleeding through the paint film. Then comes a wood primer, which may be water-based or solvent-based, followed by an undercoat and then the top coat. To speed up the painting process, paint manufacturers have now perfected combined primer/undercoats, and have also introduced so-called *self-undercoating* gloss paint which just needs a primer.

On metal, a primer is generally needed. A zinc phosphate primer is used for iron or steel, and there are special primers for aluminium. This is then followed by an undercoat and top coat, as for wood. Copper, brass and lead can be painted directly without the need for a primer so long as they are brought to a bright finish first and are thoroughly degreased with white spirit (paint thinner).

Varnishes and wood stains

Varnish is basically paint without the pigment. Most contain polyurethane resins and are solvent-based (like oil paint), although water-based acrylic varnishes are becoming more popular for health and environmental reasons,

CLEANING PAINTING EQUIPMENT

Paint is thinned or diluted if necessary with water or white spirit (paint thinner) according to the paint type. Wash tools and equipment in soapy water if using a water-based paint, and with white spirit or a proprietary brush cleaner for solvent-based (oil) paint. Soak hardened paint in paint remover overnight, then wash out the softened paint with hot soapy water.

ABOVE Coloured varnishes help to enhance the colour of the wood grain without obliterating it completely, as paint does.

ABOVE Varnish is a hardwearing alternative to paint on wood with an attractive grain pattern, and the surface shows marks less readily than paint too.

just as solvent-based paints are losing ground to water-based types. Varnishes are available with a satin/silk or a high-gloss finish, either clear or with the addition of small amounts of colour. These coloured varnishes are intended to enhance the appearance of the wood, or to give it some extra colour without obliterating the wood grain, as paint would do.

Varnish is its own primer and undercoat, although it is best to thin the first coat with about 10 per cent white spirit (paint thinner) for solvent-based types, or water for acrylic types, and to apply it with a lint-free cloth rather than a brush so that it can be rubbed well into the wood grain. When this first coat has dried, it is *keyed* or roughened by rubbing very lightly with fine abrasive paper (sandpaper), dusted off, and a second, full-strength coat brushed on. For surfaces likely to get a lot of wear, it is advisable to key the second coat as before and apply an additional coat.

Wood stains, unlike paint and varnish, are designed to soak into the wood. They may subsequently be sealed

with clear varnish to improve the finish and make the surface more durable. They are available in water-based or solvent-based types in a wide range of colours and wood shades; different colours of the same type can be blended to obtain intermediate shades, and the stain can be thinned with water or white spirit as appropriate to give a paler effect.

Stains are often applied with a brush or a paint pad, but it is often quicker and easier to get even coverage by putting them on with a clean lint-free cloth. Quick work is needed to blend wet edges together, and to avoid overlaps which will leave darker patches as the stain dries. A water-based stain will raise fibres on the surface of the wood, which will spoil the evenness of the colour. The solution is to sand the surface perfectly smooth first and then dampen it with a wet cloth. This will raise the surface fibres. When the wood is dry these fibres are sanded off with extra-fine abrasive paper, ready to receive the application of stain.

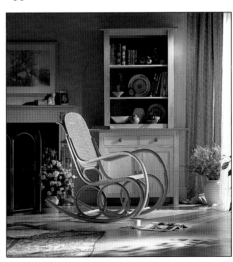

ABOVE Varnish can be used to enhance the natural beauty of wood throughout the home, from floors and fire surrounds to storage units and other items of furniture.

PAINTING TOOLS AND EQUIPMENT

Two groups of tools are needed, one for preparing the surface and one for actually putting the paint on. For a masonry wall, the minimum preparation is to wash down any previously painted surface. This calls for a bucket, sponges and cloths, strong household detergent or sugar soap (all-purpose cleaner), and rubber gloves to protect the hands.

If the washed-down surface has a high-gloss finish, or feels rough to the touch, use fine abrasive paper (sandpaper) and a sanding block to smooth it down. Wet-and-dry (silicon carbide) paper, used wet, is best for sanding down existing paintwork; rinse off the resulting fine slurry of paint with water afterwards. Use ordinary abrasive paper for bare wood.

Defects in the surface need filling. Use a traditional cellulose filler (spackle) for small cracks, chips and other surface blemishes, and an expanding filler foam which can be shaped and sanded when hard for larger defects. To apply filler paste use a filling knife (putty knife).

To strip existing paintwork, use either a heat gun – easier to control and much safer to use than a blowtorch – or a chemical paint remover, plus scrapers of various shapes to remove the softened paint. For removing wall coverings in order to apply a painted wall or ceiling finish, a steam wallpaper stripper will be invaluable. The small all-in-one strippers which resemble a large steam iron are the easiest type to use.

Painting tools

The paintbrush is still the favourite tool for applying paint to walls, ceilings, woodwork and metalwork around the house. Most are made with natural bristle, held in a metal ferrule which is attached to a wooden or plastic handle, but there are also brushes with synthetic fibre bristles which are sometimes recommended for applying water-based (latex) paints.

Brushes come in widths from 12 mm (½ in) up to 150 mm (6 in). The smallest sizes are used for fiddly jobs such as painting glazing bars (muntins), while the widest are ideal for flat uninterrupted wall and ceiling surfaces. However, a wide brush can be tiring to use, especially with solvent-based (oil) paints. There are also long-handled

PREPARATION EQUIPMENT

The following tools and equipment are the general items needed to prepare for repainting: steam wallpaper stripper (**1**), liquid paint remover (**2**), paste paint remover (**3**), cellulose filler (spackle) (**4**), expanding filler foam (**5**), rubber gloves (**6**), bucket (**7**), sugar soap (all-purpose cleaner) (**8**), sponge (**9**), cloth (**10**), spray gun (**11**), abrasive paper (sandpaper) (**12**), sanding block (**13**), shavehooks (triangular scrapers) (**14**), scrapers (**15**), heat gun and attachments (a directional nozzle and two integral scrapers) (**16**).

brushes with angled heads for painting behind radiators, and narrow brushes called *cutting-in* (sash) brushes, which have the bristle tips cut off at an angle for painting into internal angles. For the best results, buy good-quality brushes and look after them, rather than buy cheap ones and throw them away after finishing the job.

Paint rollers are used mainly for painting walls and ceilings with water-based paints, although they can be used with solvent-based types too. They consist of a metal roller cage mounted on a handle, plus a hollow sleeve that fits onto the cage and actually applies the paint. Some can be fitted with an extension pole, which is useful if there are high ceilings or stairwells to paint. Most rollers are 180 mm (7 in) wide;

larger sizes are available, but can be harder to 'drive'. There are also slim mini-rollers for painting awkward-to-reach areas such as walls behind radiators. For any type, a roller tray is used to load paint onto the sleeve. Solid water-based paint is sold in its own tray.

The sleeves are waterproof tubes with a layer of foam plastic or cloth stuck to the outside. The second type may be made from natural or synthetic fibre, and have a short, medium or long pile. Choose the pile length to match the surface being painted: short for flat surfaces, medium for those with a slight texture and long for heavily embossed or sculpted surfaces.

Paint pads are squares or rectangles of short-pile cloth stuck to a foam backing

and mounted on a plastic or metal handle. The pad is dipped in a shallow container, or loaded from a special paint container with a roller feed, and then drawn across the surface. Pads come in a range of sizes.

Paint and varnish are also sold in *aerosol* form. This is ideal for small areas or fiddly materials such as wickerwork, but too expensive to use on large areas.

Lastly, do not forget the decorating sundries. A *paint kettle* is needed for decanting the paint and straining out any foreign bodies. Hand-held *paint masks* or *masking tape* are invaluable aids to getting straight edges and keeping paint off adjacent surfaces. Above all, remember to provide *dust sheets* (drop cloths), which perform better than plastic sheets.

PAINTING EQUIPMENT

This selection of equipment includes: brushes in various sizes (**1**), aerosol paint (**2**), long-handled brush for use behind radiators (**3**), hand-held skirting (baseboard) masks (**4**), slimline mini-roller (**5**), roller extension pole (**6**), a full-sized roller with short-pile sleeve and roller tray (**7**), dust sheet (drop cloth) (**8**), white spirit (paint thinner) (**9**), long pile and textured roller sleeves (**10**), paint shield (**11**), masking tape (**12**), paint kettle (**13**), paint pads in various sizes and shapes (**14**), paint-loading containers for paint pads (**15**).

PATCHING WALL AND CEILING DAMAGE

Plasterboard (gypsum board) is an immensely versatile material for lining walls and ceilings, since it provides a smooth surface for any finish and has useful sound-deadening and fireproofing properties. The one thing it does not do very well is to resist impacts, and the resulting hole cannot simply be patched with filler because the board's strength has been lost at the point of damage. The solution is either to strengthen the board or to replace a section altogether.

Very small holes can be disguised with self-adhesive scrim tape and cellulose filler (spackle), but holes more than about 50 mm (2 in) across need a more substantial repair. Use an offcut of plasterboard and cut a piece slightly narrower than the hole width and twice as long as its height to use as a patch. Pierce a hole in it, thread a piece of string through, tie one end to a nail and pull this against the face of the patch. Then butter some plaster or filler onto the other face of the patch and push it into the hole, keeping hold of the string with the other hand. Position the patch against the inner face of the plasterboard, pulling on the string to help the filler stick it in place. When it has stuck fast, fill the hole and cut off the string.

For larger holes – a foot through the ceiling, for example – in plasterboard and (in older properties) lath-and-plaster surfaces, the only solution is to cut out the damaged piece and nail on a new section in its place. Supports will need to be fixed around the edges of the opening where the damaged section has been cut out. Then fill the cut edges, apply joint tape to hide them and skim over the patch with a little plaster to complete the repair.

PATCHING SMALL HOLES IN PLASTERBOARD (GYPSUM BOARD)

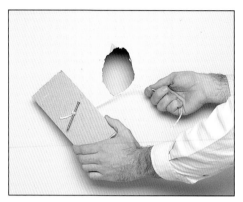

1 Cut a plasterboard patch slightly longer and narrower than the hole, and thread a length of string with a nail tied on through a hole in its centre.

2 Butter some plaster or filler onto the edges of the patch and feed it end-on into the hole, keeping hold of the string with the other hand.

3 Pull the string to hold the patch against the rear face of the board, then fill the recess with plaster or filler and cut off the string.

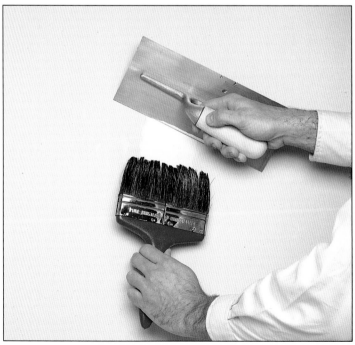

4 Complete the repair by applying a skim coat of plaster over the patch. Flick water onto it with a brush and polish it smooth with a float.

PATCHING LARGER HOLES IN PLASTERBOARD (GYPSUM BOARD)

1 If the plasterboard surface is more extensively damaged, cut through it with a sharp knife back to the adjacent wall studs or ceiling joists.

2 Cut across to the stud or joist centres, then make two vertical cuts down the centre of the stud or joist to free the damaged panel.

3 Cut two strips of wood to fit between the studs/joists, and screw or nail them into place so they will support the edges of the main board and the patch.

4 Cut a plasterboard patch to match the section removed, and nail it into place. Fill and tape the joints and skim plaster over the repair to conceal it.

REPAIRING LATH-AND-PLASTER SURFACES

1 If the wood laths are split or broken, pull them away from the surface. Remove any loose sections of plaster from around the site of the damage.

2 Continue cutting back the old plaster and the laths behind it to expose the studs or ceiling joists at each side of the hole. Square off the edges.

3 Cut a plasterboard patch to fit the hole, and nail it in place. Add two support strips as described for patching plasterboard if the panel is large.

4 Complete the repair by plastering over the patch after filling and taping the cut edges all around. Polish the repair with a steel float.

PREPARING SURFACES FOR PAINTING

Modern paints have excellent adhesion and covering power, but to get the best performance from them they must be given a good start by preparing the surface thoroughly.

Wash surfaces, which have previously been painted, using a solution of strong household detergent or sugar soap (all-purpose cleaner). Rinse them very thoroughly with clean water, and allow them to dry completely before starting repainting.

Remove areas of flaking paint with a scraper or filling knife (putty knife), and then either touch in the bare area with more paint or fill it flush with the surrounding paint film by using fine filler (spackle). Sand this smooth when it has hardened.

If the surface shows signs of mildew growth due to persistent condensation, wipe it over with household bleach, or refrigerator cleaner containing a fungicide, to kill off the spores. Wash down the surface with detergent and rinse thoroughly.

If knots are showing through on painted woodwork, sand the paint film back to bare wood and apply knotting (shellac) to the knot, then prime and undercoat to bring the new paint film level with the surrounding paintwork. Sand between coats. Resinous knots may produce stains which can only be prevented by drying the knot out with a blowtorch.

PREPARING PAINTED WOODWORK

1 Use fine-grade abrasive paper (sandpaper) wrapped around a sanding block to remove 'nibs' from the paint surface and to key the paint film ready for repainting.

2 Wash the surface down with detergent or sugar soap (all-purpose cleaner) to remove dirt, grease, finger marks and the dust from sanding it. Rinse with clean water, ensuring that no detergent residue is left as this will inhibit the new paint film.

3 Use a proprietary tack rag or a clean cloth moistened with white spirit (paint thinner) to remove dust from recessed mouldings and other awkward corners.

FILLING DEFECTS IN WOOD

1 Fill splits and dents in wood using filler (spackle) on painted surfaces, and tinted wood stopper (patcher) on new or stripped wood that will be varnished.

2 Use the corner of a filling knife (putty knife), or even a finger, to work the filler into recesses and other awkward-to-reach places. Smooth off excess filler before it dries.

3 When the filler or wood stopper has hardened completely, use abrasive paper (sandpaper) wrapped around a sanding block to sand the repair down flush.

FILLING CRACKS IN PLASTER

1 Use the corner of a filling knife (putty knife) to rake out loose material along the line of the crack, and to undercut the edges slightly so that the filler has a better grip.

2 Brush out dust and debris from the crack, using an old paintbrush. Alternatively, use the crevice nozzle attachment of a vacuum cleaner.

3 Dampen the surrounding plaster with water from a garden spray gun to prevent it from drying out the filler too quickly and causing it to crack.

4 Mix up some filler on a plasterer's hawk (mortarboard) or a board offcut to a firm consistency. Alternatively, use ready-mixed filler or wallboard compound.

5 Use a filling knife to press the filler well into the crack, drawing the blade across it and then along it. Aim to leave the repair slightly proud.

DEALING WITH STAINS

If ceilings have been stained by plumbing leaks, seal the affected area with a proprietary aerosol stain sealer to prevent the stain from showing through the new paint film. Alternatively, paint the affected area with white gloss (oil) paint – it will seal just as well and is usually already on hand. It can be overpainted with water-based (latex) paint.

6 When the filler has hardened, use fine-grade abrasive paper (sandpaper) wrapped around a sanding block to smooth the repair flush with the surrounding wall.

STRIPPING PAINT

Every time a surface is repainted, this adds a little more thickness to the paint layer. It does not matter much on wall or ceiling surfaces, but on woodwork (and, to a lesser extent, on metalwork) this build-up of successive layers of paint can eventually lead to the clogging of detail on mouldings. More importantly, moving parts such as doors and windows start to bind and catch against their frames. If this happens, it is time to strip off the paint back to bare wood and build up a new paint system from scratch.

It may also be necessary to strip an old paint finish if it is in such poor condition – from physical damage, for example – that repainting will no longer cover up the faults adequately.

There are two methods of removing paint from wood and metal surfaces. The first is using *heat*, traditionally from a blowtorch but nowadays more often an electric heat gun. The second is to use a *chemical paint remover*, which contains either dimethylene chloride or caustic soda. Heat works well on wood, but may scorch the surface and can crack the glass in windows; it is less successful on metal because the material conducts heat away as it is applied. Chemicals work well on all surfaces, but need handling with care; always follow the manufacturer's instructions to the letter.

HOMEMADE PASTE REMOVER

Add caustic soda to water until no more will dissolve. Thicken to a paste with oatmeal and use as for proprietary paste remover. Be particularly careful when using this corrosive solution. If it splashes on the skin, rinse at once with plenty of cold water.

USING A HEAT GUN

1 Play the air stream from the heat gun over the surface to soften the paint film. Scrape it off as it bubbles up, and deposit the hot scrapings in an old metal container.

2 Use a shavehook (triangular scraper) instead of a flat scraper to remove the paint from mouldings. Take care not to scorch the wood if it is to be varnished afterwards.

3 Remove any remnants of paint from the wood surface with wire wool soaked in white spirit (paint thinner), working along the direction of the grain.

4 Use a hand vacuum cleaner to remove any remaining loose particles of paint from the crevices in mouldings and from any other inaccessible areas.

5 Sand the surface of the wood lightly to remove any raised fibres or rough patches, then wipe it over with a clean cloth moistened with white spirit.

6 Seal the resin in any exposed knots by brushing on a coat of liquid knotting (shellac). Leave this to dry thoroughly before priming the wood.

7 Apply a coat of either wood primer or a combined primer/undercoat to the stripped wood surface to provide optimum adhesion for the subsequent top coats.

USING LIQUID REMOVER

1 Wear rubber gloves and old clothing. Decant the liquid into a polythene (polyethylene) container or an old can, then brush it onto the surface you want to strip. Leave it until the paint film bubbles up.

2 Use a flat scraper or shavehook (triangular scraper) as appropriate to remove the softened paint. Deposit the scrapings safely in an old container.

3 Neutralize the stripper by washing the surface down with water or white spirit (paint thinner), as recommended by the manufacturer. Leave it to dry.

USING PASTE REMOVER

1 Paste removers are especially good for removing paint from intricate mouldings because they dry very slowly. Apply the paste liberally to the surface.

2 Give the paste plenty of time to work, especially on thick paint layers. Then scrape it off and wash down the surface with plenty of water to neutralize the chemical.

USING A PAINTBRUSH

The paintbrush is the most versatile and therefore the most widely used tool for applying paint. Choose the brush size to match the surface being painted. For example, for painting glazing bars (muntins) on windows or narrow mouldings on a door, use a slim brush – or perhaps a cutting-in (sash) brush if painting up to an adjacent unpainted surface such as glass where a neat edge to the paint film is needed. For expansive, flat areas select a larger brush for quick coverage. Remember that the largest wall brushes can be tiring to use, especially with solvent-based (oil) paints.

Get rid of any loose bristles in a new brush by flicking it vigorously across the palm of the hand before using it for the first time. Wash previously used brushes that have been stored unwrapped to remove any dust or other debris from the bristles, and leave them to dry out again before using them to apply a solvent-based paint.

Always check that the metal ferrule is securely attached to the brush handle, and hammer in any projecting nails or staples. Check too that the ferrule is free from rust which could discolour the paint. To remove rust use either wire wool or abrasive paper (sandpaper).

PREPARING THE PAINT

1 Wipe the lid first to remove any dust. Then prise it off with a wide lever such as the thicker edge of a table knife to avoid damage to the lip.

2 Decant some paint into a clean metal or plastic paint kettle, or small bucket. This is easier to handle than a full container, especially one without a handle.

3 Remove any paint skin from partly used containers. Then strain the paint into the paint kettle through a piece of old stocking or tights (pantyhose), or cheesecloth.

HOLDING THE BRUSH

1 Before using a new brush, work it vigorously backwards and forwards across the palm of the hand to remove any loose bristles. Wash stored brushes.

2 The best control of a small or medium-sized brush is achieved by holding it with the fingers and thumb on the ferrule, rather than on the handle.

3 Wide wall brushes can be tiring to use, and it is usually more comfortable to grip the brush by the handle rather than by the ferrule.

1 To load the brush with paint, dip it into the paint to about a third of the bristle depth. An overloaded brush will cause drips, and paint will run down the brush handle.

2 Tie a length of string or wire across the mouth of the paint kettle between the handle supports, and use it to scrape excess paint from the bristles.

3 Apply the paint to the wood in long, sweeping strokes, brushing the paint out along the grain direction until the brush begins to run dry.

4 Load up the brush with more paint and apply it to the next area. Blend the two together with short, light strokes, again along the grain direction.

5 Repeat this process while working across the area, blending the edges of adjacent areas together with light brushstrokes to avoid leaving a visible join.

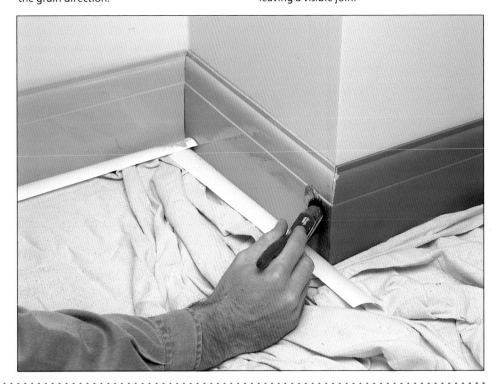

6 At edges and external corners, let the brush run off the edge to avoid a build-up of paint on the corner. Repeat the process for the opposite edge.

USING PAINT ROLLERS AND PADS

Paint rollers are generally used to apply water-based (latex) paints to large, flat areas such as walls and ceilings. Choose a sleeve with a short pile for painting plaster, a medium pile for painting embossed or textured wall coverings, and a long pile for deeply sculpted surfaces such as those created with textured finishes (texture paints). Rollers can also apply solvent-based (oil) paint to flat surfaces such as flush doors, but tend to leave a distinctive 'orange peel' texture rather than the smooth finish left by a paintbrush.

There are some drawbacks with paint rollers: they cannot paint right up to internal corners or wall/ceiling angles, so these need to be painted first with a brush or pad. They can also splash if 'driven' too fast, and the sleeves take a lot of time and effort to clean thoroughly, especially if they have been used for a long period and there is dried paint in the pile. Repeated cleaning eventually causes the sleeve to peel from its core.

People either love or loathe paint pads. They tend to apply less paint per coat than either a brush or a roller, so an additional coat may be needed in some circumstances, but they make it easy to apply paint smoothly and evenly with no risk of brush marks.

USING A ROLLER

1 Select a sleeve with the required fibre type and pile length, and slide it onto the sprung metal cage until it meets the stop next to the handle.

2 Decant some paint (previously strained if from an old can) into the roller tray until the paint level just laps up the sloping section.

3 Brush a band of paint about 50 mm (2 in) wide into internal corners and wall/ceiling angles, around doors and windows, and above skirtings (baseboards).

4 Load the roller sleeve with paint by running it down the sloping section into the paint. Then roll it up and down the slope to remove the excess.

5 Start applying the paint in a series of overlapping diagonal strokes to ensure complete coverage of the surface. Continue until the sleeve runs dry.

6 Reload the sleeve and tackle the next section in the same way. Finish off by blending the areas together, working parallel to corners and edges.

USING A PAINT PAD

1 Pour some paint into the special applicator tray. Then load the pad by running it backwards and forwards over the ridged loading roller.

2 On walls, apply the paint in a series of overlapping parallel bands. Use a small pad or a special edging pad (see step 4) to paint right up to corners or angles.

3 Use smaller pads for painting narrow areas such as mouldings on doors or glazing bars (muntins) on windows, brushing out the paint along the direction of the grain.

4 Special edging pads are designed for painting right up to internal angles, and have small wheels which guide the pad along the adjacent surface as you work.

USING AEROSOL PAINT

Aerosol paints and varnishes are ideal for hard-to-decorate surfaces such as wickerwork. Always follow the maker's instructions when using them.

5 Some larger pads can be fitted to an extension pole to make it easier to paint ceilings and high walls. Make sure the pad is attached securely.

PAINTING

PAINTING WALLS AND CEILINGS

Paint is a popular decorative finish for walls and ceilings because it is quick and easy to apply, offers a huge range of colours and is relatively inexpensive compared with rival products such as wall coverings. It can be used over plain plaster, or can be applied over embossed relief wall coverings and textured finishes.

Before starting painting, clear the room and prepare the surfaces. Start by taking down curtains and blinds (drapes and shades). Remove furniture to another room if possible, or else group it in the middle of the room and cover it with clear plastic sheeting. Take down lampshades and pendant light fittings (after turning off the power supply). Unscrew wall-mounted fittings and remove the hardware from doors and windows if they are being repainted at the same time.

Protect surfaces not being repainted, such as wall switches and socket outlets (receptacles), with masking tape. Finally, cover the floor with dust sheets (drop cloths), which will absorb paint splashes; vacuum-clean surfaces such as window sills, picture rails and skirtings (baseboards) where dust can settle, and turn off forced-air heating so that dust is not recirculated into the room.

Access equipment

Normally most of the surfaces to be painted can be reached from a standing or a kneeling position, but for ceilings, the tops of room walls and the upper reaches of stairwells some access equipment is needed. A simple stepladder, ideally with a top platform big enough to support a paint kettle or roller tray, will be adequate for painting walls and ceilings.

Paint walls and ceilings in a series of overlapping bands. Start painting the ceiling next to the window wall so that reflected light on the wet paint shows whether coverage is even. On walls, right-handed people should work from right to left, and left-handed people the other way.

For stairwells, use steps or ladder sections plus secured scaffold boards or the components of a slot-together access tower to set up a work platform that allows you to get to all the surfaces without over-reaching.

Texture paints

Texture paints are water-based (latex) paints thickened with added fillers. Once the paint has been applied to the decorating surface, a range of three-dimensional effects can be created using various patterning or texturing techniques. These paints are ideal for covering up surfaces in poor condition. Most are white, but they can be overpainted with ordinary water-based paint for a coloured effect. Avoid using them in kitchens – the textured surface will trap dirt and grease which is difficult to clean.

PAINT COVERAGE

Paint coverage depends on several factors, including the roughness and porosity of the surface to which it is being applied and the thickness of the coating. For example, the first coat of paint will soak into new plaster, so the coverage will be less than is achieved with subsequent coats. Similarly, a textured surface will hold more paint than a smooth one, again reducing the paint coverage.

The figures given here are intended as a rough guide only. Always check the manufacturer's coverage figure on the container, and use that plus the area to be painted to work out how much paint is required.

ESTIMATING QUANTITIES

Paint type	Sq m per litre	Sq ft per gallon
Liquid gloss (oil) paint	16	650
Non-drip gloss paint	13	530
Eggshell	12	490
Matt (flat) water-based (latex) paint	15	610
Silk (satin) water-based paint	14	570
Non-drip water-based paint	12	490
Undercoat	11	450
Wood primer	12	490
Metal primer	10	410
Varnish	15–20	610–820

USING TEXTURE PAINT

1 Start applying the paint to the wall or ceiling surface in a series of overlapping random strokes, recharging the roller or brush at intervals.

2 When an area of about 1 sq m (11 sq ft) is covered, go over the whole area with a series of parallel roller/brush strokes for an even surface texture.

3 Give the textured finish the look of tree bark by drawing a flat-bladed scraper or similar edged tool over the surface to flatten off the high spots.

4 Use a texturing comb to create overlapping swirls, working across the area. Practise the effect on paint applied to a piece of heavy cardboard first.

5 Twist a sponge before pulling it away from the wall surface to create a series of small, overlapping swirls in the paint finish. Rinse the sponge regularly.

6 You can buy patterning roller sleeves in a range of different designs for use with texture paints. This one creates a regular diamond pattern.

7 This patterning sleeve gives a random streaked effect when rolled down the wall. Apply the texture paint with a brush first if using a patterning sleeve.

SPECIAL PAINT EFFECTS

There is no need to stick to plain colour on painted walls as there is a wide range of special paint effects that will enliven their looks. Some of these effects are purely decorative in their own right; others imitate the appearance of other materials. All can be created with the use of inexpensive tools and materials, and practice and patience will bring highly attractive results.

The special paint effects dealt with here fall into two broad groups: *broken colour* and *imitation*. In the first group a range of different techniques is used to apply a second colour over a different base colour so that the latter still shows through, providing a pleasing two-colour effect. In the second group paint is used to copy the looks of materials such as wood veneers and marble.

For either finish it is essential to prepare the surface of the wall or woodwork thoroughly first (see chart).

Glazes

Most special effects are applied as a tinted glaze which is semi-transparent and allows the underlying base colour to show through. Water-based glazes are made from water-based (latex) paint diluted with water or a proprietary emulsion glaze until the required level of translucency has been achieved. Use coloured paints or tint white paint to the required shade with artists' acrylics. Water-based glazes produce a thinner, more open, coat of colour and they dry extremely quickly, which means they are not suitable for the more complex special paint effects.

Scumble is the main component of solvent-based (oil) glazes and is generally diluted with a mixture of 1 part linseed oil to 2 parts white spirit (paint thinner). However, the proportions can be varied: a higher proportion of scumble will increase the definition of the effect and will retard the drying time; more linseed oil produces a smoother texture; white spirit thins the glaze and speeds up the drying time. Once the glaze has been mixed, pour off a small quantity and add the colour to this, using either eggshell paint or artists' oils. When the correct colour has been mixed, gradually add this to the main quantity of glaze until the required level of transparency is achieved. Solvent-based glazes have a rich, hardwearing

TOOLS AND MATERIALS

Among the tools and materials needed are a stencilling brush (**1**), a dusting brush (**2**), a small paintbrush (**3**), a softening brush (**4**), a stippling brush (**5**), artists' paintbrushes (**6**), cotton or linen rags (**7**), a natural marine sponge (**8**), a rubber rocker for graining (**9**), a large paintbrush (**10**) and a flat-bristle varnishing brush (**11**).

finish and the slower drying times are particularly suited to special effects.

If working over large areas – more than 2 sq m (22 sq ft) – two people will be needed to achieve the best finish: one to apply the glaze and the other to work it. This is the only way to maintain a wet edge and therefore to avoid noticeable joins between one area of colour and the next.

Stencilling

This is slightly different from the other techniques, since the stencil produces a clearly defined shape. It is very simple to do, and can be used to create effects in more than one colour by using different stencils. Ready-cut stencils can be bought, but it is easy to create designs of your own.

PREPARING SURFACES

The method of preparation varies depending on whether water-based (latex) paints or solvent-based (oil) paints are used for the final effect. Care taken at this early stage will help to ensure a satisfying end result.

Once the preparation is complete, apply the chosen base colour. Use eggshell for a good opaque and non-porous surface if using either a water- or a solvent-based finish and, when dry, rub it down with fine abrasive paper (sandpaper).

Surface	Water-based effect	Solvent-based effect
Bare plaster	Prime with diluted water-based paint	Prime with proprietary primer or PVA adhesive (white glue)
	Apply 1–2 water-based undercoats	Apply 1–2 solvent-based undercoats
Painted plaster	Wash down, repair defects and sand solvent-based finishes	Wash down, repair defects and sand solvent-based finishes
	Apply 1–2 water-based undercoats	Apply 1–2 solvent-based undercoats
Hardboard	Prime with diluted water-based paint	Prime with proprietary primer
	Apply 1–2 water-based undercoats	Apply 1–2 solvent-based undercoats
Bare wood	Apply knotting (shellac) to knots	Apply knotting (shellac) to knots
	Prime with diluted water-based paint	Apply proprietary primer
	Apply 1–2 water-based undercoats	Apply 1–2 solvent-based undercoats
Painted wood	As for Painted plaster	As for Painted plaster
Varnished wood	Strip and prepare as for Bare wood	Strip and prepare as for Bare wood

CUTTING STENCILS

To cut stencils, tracing paper, some special waxed paper for stencils (available from art stores), a pencil, a pin and a scalpel or sharp utility knife are needed. Trace or draw the pattern and enlarge or reduce it on a photocopier, if necessary. Tape the finished trace to the stencil paper and prick through it to mark the design outline on the stencil paper. Join up the prick marks in pencil. Alternatively, transfer the trace onto the stencil using carbon paper. Cut out the design carefully, leaving sufficient ties to bridge the separate areas of the design. Allow a large margin above and below the design so that the stencil is sufficiently strong. Reinforce any tears or accidental cuts with adhesive tape.

1 Affix the stencil to the surface with masking tape, aligning it with a true horizontal pencil guideline. Dip the stencilling brush in the paint and remove the excess on some waste paper. Use a pouncing action to apply the paint to minimize the risk of colour seeping under the stencil and marring the masked-off areas.

2 When the paint is touch-dry, release the stencil, wipe off the wet paint and reposition it farther along the wall to create the next section of the pattern.

Sponging

This technique involves dabbing irregular patches of paint onto the base coat. Two or more different sponged colours can be applied. Note that a natural marine sponge must be used to create this effect; man-made sponges do not work. Soak it in water first until it swells to its full size, then wring it out ready to start applying the paint.

1 After testing the effect on an offcut of board, dip the sponge in the paint and apply light pressure to leave overlapping splodges of colour.

2 Allow the first application to dry, then go over the surface again and add more colour if necessary to deepen the contrast with the base colour.

3 If applying a different second colour, allow the first colour to dry and then use the same technique to apply the new colour over it.

Rag-rolling

Another simple two-colour effect, rag-rolling involves brushing a diluted second colour over the base coat and then using a rolled-up 'sausage' of cloth to remove some of the second colour before it starts to dry.

The technique works best with a base coat of eggshell paint and a top coat of eggshell paint diluted with white spirit (paint thinner). Use lint-free cotton or linen rags and change them frequently before they become soaked with paint.

1 Allow the base coat to dry thoroughly. Then lightly brush on the second diluted colour in bands across the surface, aiming to leave a random pattern of brushstrokes that allows the base colour to show through.

2 Roll the rag sausage across the surface in a continuous motion. Vary the direction for a random effect and touch in small areas by just dabbing with the cloth. Replace the rag regularly.

Stippling

For an attractive mottled appearance, try stippling; apart from being used as a decorative finish in its own right it can also be used to obliterate brush marks in the base coat beneath other broken-colour effects.

The one item of specialist equipment that is needed to create this effect is a stippling brush.

1 Brush the glaze on over the base coat, applying a generous coat. Do not worry about leaving brush marks; the stippling will obliterate them.

2 Hold the stippling brush with the bristle tips parallel with the surface, and simply hit the paint film. Clean paint from the brush regularly, wiping it with a dry cloth.

Colour washing

This is one of the simplest broken-colour effects. Brush on the glaze and then use a dry softening brush or an ordinary wide paintbrush to create a random pattern of brushstrokes that allow the base coat to show through. A further colour can be added.

1 Brush a liberal coat of the glaze over the base coat. The effect of colour washing is enhanced when there is a good contrast between the two paint colours.

2 Draw the softening brush over the glaze in a series of long random strokes in varying directions. Add a further toning colour if desired when this coat has dried.

Graining

Graining is a technique that aims to imitate the look of natural wood, especially the more exotic and expensive species. Use a solvent-based (oil) eggshell paint for the base coat, and a solvent-based glaze.

1 Brush the glaze onto the wood surface, leaving the brush marks visible along the direction of the intended wood grain effect.

2 Then, after a couple of minutes, draw a dry graining brush or an ordinary paintbrush lightly over the glaze to create the actual grain pattern.

3 Use a rubber rocker (as here), a graining comb or a bristle grainer to produce the individual grain characteristics of the wood you are copying.

Dragging

Another very simple effect, dragging is created by drawing a dry brush over the glaze in a series of parallel strokes that allow the base colour to show through. Use a normal paintbrush in a width to suit the surface being decorated.

1 Brush a generous coat of glaze over the base coat. Always work parallel to the direction of the grain if applying the effect to wood.

2 Use a dry paintbrush to drag a series of parallel lines in the second colour. Wipe the build-up of paint off the brush at regular intervals with a dry cloth.

Marbling

As its name implies, marbling copies the appearance of marble. It is a relatively difficult technique to master, but the results can be quite spectacular. For a first attempt choose a piece of real marble to copy. For best results work with a solvent-based (oil) glaze, applied over an eggshell base coat. Add the veining details with artists' oils.

1 Either brush out the glaze or apply it with a pad of lint-free cloth. Only a relatively thin coat is needed.

2 Use a dusting brush as here or a stippling brush to stipple the surface of the wet glaze. Add more colour to the glaze mixture, apply selectively to some areas for contrast and stipple the glaze again.

3 Working on the wet glaze, draw in the main areas of veining with an artists' paintbrush and a mixture of glaze and artists' oils. Use different weights of line to create a natural-looking effect.

4 Use the softening brush again to soften the outlines of the veining and to blend it into the background. Wipe the brush regularly to avoid smudges.

VARNISHING SPECIAL PAINT EFFECTS

Some special paint effects, especially graining and marbling, should be sealed with a coat of clear varnish once the effect has dried completely. Use satin varnish rather than gloss unless a particularly polished effect is required. When this has dried, burnish the surface with a soft cloth and add a little wax polish to create a realistic surface sheen, if wished.

5 Highlight some areas of the veining by adding more colour or a second colour. Soften the effect again, as in step 4.

PAPERHANGING

The term 'wall coverings' is used to describe the whole range of decorative materials sold in roll form and designed to be stuck to wall and ceiling surfaces with a strippable adhesive. The range includes an enormous variety of designs, patterns and colourways . . . almost too many, as any home decorator will testify when confronted by an array of pattern books and trying to decide which covering to select.

The vast majority of wall coverings are either made entirely from paper, or have a plastic or cloth layer bonded to a paper backing so that they can be hung in the same way as all-paper types. The basic technology of paperhanging has changed little over the centuries, even if the products have been subtly altered and improved; people still paper the living room in a way that would be familiar to their grandparents.

The two main developments that have occurred in recent years are the introduction of ready-pasted types which are immersed in a trough of water instead of having paste brushed onto them, and of all-plastic wall coverings which are hung by pasting the wall.

This chapter gives information on the various types of wall covering available and on the tools, materials and other equipment needed to hang or strip them. There is advice on how to go about removing existing wall decorations – other wall coverings, materials such as texture paints, wall panelling and tiles of various types – and on preparing the surface. This is followed by detailed step-by-step instructions on how to hang a new wall covering on walls and ceilings, and on how to cope with awkward areas such as door and window openings, arches and stairwells.

OPPOSITE
There is virtually no limit to the versatility of modern wall coverings. This complementary match of broken colour and simple stripes is linked by a striking multicoloured border at dado (chair) rail level.

TYPES OF WALL COVERING

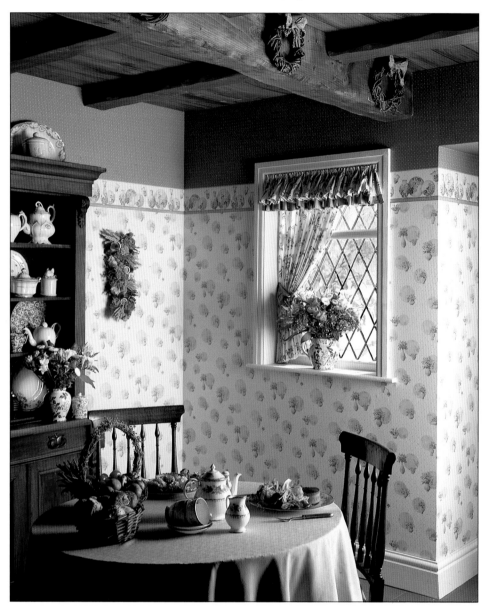

Wall coverings fall into two basic groups: those with a printed design or a surface material which is decorative in its own right, and those with a surface texture or embossing which are designed to be painted over once they have been hung.

Printed wallpaper is exactly that – paper with a coloured design printed on it. It may also be embossed along the lines of the design, or may have a distinctive surface texture added during manufacture. Cheaper types may be awkward to hang, tearing easily or stretching so as to make accurate pattern matching difficult. More expensive types, especially hand-printed ones, are better in this respect, but care must still be taken when hanging them to keep paste off the face of the paper. The strongest printed wallpapers are called *duplex papers*, and are made by bonding two layers of paper together during the manufacturing process. Most printed papers can be wiped with a damp cloth if they become stained, but it is wise to check whether this is the case when selecting this type of wall covering. All are easy to strip, making them a good choice if you like to redecorate regularly.

Washable wallpaper is a printed wallpaper which has a thin clear plastic coating applied over the design during manufacture to render it water and stain resistant. As with printed types, the surface may be embossed or textured. Washable wallpapers are also widely available in ready-pasted form. The plastic surface will withstand gentle washing and sponging with a mild detergent, but not prolonged scrubbing or the use of abrasive cleaners. Choose them for rooms where they will be subject to moderate wear, or for steamy conditions such as are

LEFT Stencil borders with the design printed on a clear self-adhesive backing allow the wall covering beneath to show through – the perfect solution for unwilling stencillers.

Tougher still are the *foamed vinyl wall coverings*, which have a surface layer aerated with tiny bubbles to produce a slightly cushioned feel. The surface may be heavily textured or embossed to imitate materials such as ceramic tiles and wood grains, and is warm to the touch thanks to the insulating effect of the air bubbles – a fact that makes such a covering a good choice for rooms which are prone to mild condensation. Because of their bulk, they are

BELOW Many collections of wall coverings feature colour-coordinated borders and fabrics to enable rooms to be given the most stylish of colour treatments.

found in kitchens and bathrooms. Their main drawback is that they are difficult to remove because the plastic coating stops water penetrating and softening the paste unless it is thoroughly scored first; a steam wallpaper stripper is advisable.

Vinyl wall coverings consist of a plastic film onto which the design is printed, laminated to a paper backing. Again, the surface may also be textured or embossed, or may have a metallic appearance – the so-called *vinyl foils*. The result is a wall covering that is much tougher than a washable type; if properly hung it can be scrubbed to remove stains and marks, although care must be taken not to lift the seams by oversoaking the surface. Vinyl wall coverings are widely available in ready-pasted form, and are extremely easy to strip since the plastic layer can be peeled off dry, leaving the paper backing on the wall. They are the ideal choice for walls that will be scuffed or brushed against – in halls and landings or on staircases, for example – and also for children's rooms, kitchens and bathrooms. They are, however, more expensive than most printed or washable wall coverings, so it is just as well that they can be expected to provide excellent wear.

sometimes sold in shorter rolls than other wall coverings.

Flock wall coverings are either printed papers or vinyls with parts of the design having a raised pile – of fine wool or silk fibres on paper types and of synthetic fibres on vinyls – that closely resembles velvet. Paper types are quite delicate and must be hung with care, but vinyl flocks are extremely tough and hardwearing.

Yet another printed wall covering is made from *foamed polythene* (polyethylene) with no paper backing, and is intended to be hung by pasting

the wall and then brushing the covering into position direct from the roll – the material is very light compared to paper-backed types. The surface can be washed, but is relatively fragile and will not withstand repeated scuffing or knocks. The material can be simply dry-stripped from walls and ceilings, like the plastic surface layer of a vinyl wall covering.

An alternative to a printed surface design is a texture. This can be achieved with a paper-backed *fabric* wall covering. The commonest is hessian (burlap), but there are also

materials such as silk, tweed, wool strands, grasscloth and linen, offering a range of softly tinted or boldly coloured wall finishes. Apart from hessian, they are comparatively expensive. They can also be difficult to hang and remove, and so are best used for decorating or highlighting small and relatively well-protected areas such as alcoves. They can be vacuum-cleaned to remove surface dust, and small marks can be washed gently or lifted with special fabric cleaners.

The other kind of textured wall covering is intended for overpainting. These materials are generally known as *relief wall coverings* or 'whites'. The cheapest is *woodchip paper*, also known as oatmeal or ingrain, which has small chips of wood sandwiched at random between a heavy backing paper and a thinner surface layer. The wood chips may be fine or coarse, and the effect after painting is often likened to thinly-spread porridge.

Vinyls are also made as relief wall coverings, with a plain white aerated plastic surface layer that is moulded during manufacture into a range of random or repeating patterns.

Other relief wall coverings are embossed to produce a random or regular surface pattern. Those with a relatively low relief design are generally two-layer duplex papers which are embossed while the adhesive bonding the two layers is still wet; this helps to retain the relief during hanging. Those with more pronounced embossing are made from stronger paper containing cotton fibres rather than wood, and are also embossed wet.

All the relief wall coverings can be painted with water-based (latex) or solvent-based (oil) paints. A steam wallpaper stripper will be needed to remove them.

There is one further type of wall covering: lining (liner) paper. As its name suggests, this is a plain paper used for lining wall surfaces in poor condition or having uneven or zero porosity before a decorative wall covering is hung. It comes in various weights, from 55 g/sq m (360 lb) up to 90 g/sq m (600 lb), and in two grades, white and extra-white. The latter can also be used as an economy wall covering, and is hung in the usual way and then overpainted.

OPPOSITE Self-adhesive borders can be used to add decorative detail to any room. Here they highlight the cornice (crown molding) and form wall panels.

BELOW Borders can be used round door openings, beneath decorative features such as plate rails, and even as an unusual embellishment for panelled doors.

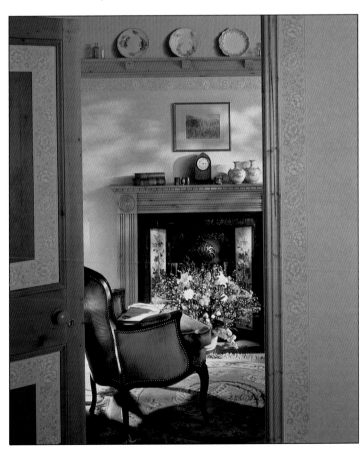

ABOVE Low-relief wallcoverings are the ideal cover-up for less-than-perfect wall surfaces, and are available in a wide range of random and regular designs.

ABOVE A three-dimensional frieze is an unusual way of filling in above a picture rail. The embossed panels are butt-jointed to form a continuous strip.

PAPERHANGING TOOLS AND EQUIPMENT

As for painting, there are two distinct groups of tools, equipment and materials to deal with wall coverings.

Stripping tools

The basic technique for removing an old wall covering is to soften the paste used to stick it to the wall so that it can be scraped off and discarded. To strip porous materials such as ordinary printed paper and the backing paper left behind after dry-stripping vinyl wall covering, use a bucket of water and a sponge or a garden spray gun to apply the water, dust sheets (drop cloths) to protect floor coverings, and a broad-bladed scraping knife to remove the softened paper.

To remove wall coverings with a water-resistant plastic or painted surface, it is necessary to pierce the surface film and so allow the water to penetrate. This can be done with a serrated wallpaper scraper or preferably a toothed roller or wheels, which is rolled backwards and forwards over the surface to create hundreds of little perforations. The water will take longer to penetrate this type of wall covering.

Stripping can be speeded up dramatically on coated wall coverings (and also on paper-backed fabrics and texture paints) by using a steam stripper. This consists of a perforated steaming plate and a water reservoir heated by electricity or bottled gas. Steam penetrates the surface far more quickly than water does, enabling the covering to be stripped quickly and effectively.

Paperhanging tools

There are four separate operations involved in hanging a new wall covering: cutting to length, pasting, hanging and trimming.

For cutting, the tools are a retractable steel tape measure, a pencil and a pair of scissors (or a sharp utility knife and a steel straightedge).

For pasting the wall covering, there should be a bucket in which to mix the paste (unless using ready-mixed tub paste), plus a stirrer and a brush with which to apply the paste. A 100 mm (4 in) wide paintbrush is satisfactory, but a special pasting brush can be bought.

As far as choosing the correct paste is concerned, follow the instructions for the wall covering concerned. In particular, remember that a paste containing a fungicide should be used for washable and vinyl coverings, to prevent mould from growing in the paste as it slowly dries under the impervious covering. A special overlap adhesive will be needed for lap joints in internal and external corners when using washables or vinyls.

When hanging a ready-pasted wall covering, the table, bucket and brush can be dispensed with. All that is needed is a plastic soaking trough in which to immerse the rolled-up lengths of wall covering.

Before starting hanging, a plumb bob and line are needed to mark a true vertical line on the wall against which to hang the first length.

Most wall coverings are applied with a special soft-bristled paperhanging brush. These are generally between 190 and 250 mm (7½ to 10 in) wide, and have a slim handle. The soft bristles help to make the wall covering follow the contours of the wall surface behind, and also eliminate undue hand contact with the face of the covering, which might mark it.

A sponge can be used instead of a brush for hanging washables or vinyls, especially if they are ready-pasted, since here the sponge helps mop water from the surface of the wall covering as well as smoothing it into place.

The final stage is trimming, and the best tool for this is a special pair of paperhangers' scissors. These have blades up to 300 mm (12 in) long for making long, straight cuts.

For papering walls a stepladder is needed which should be tall enough to enable the ceiling to be easily touched. For papering ceilings, set up a proper platform across the width of the room at a comfortable height, using scaffold boards or staging on trestles or other low supports to ensure complete stability. Do not step from chair to chair or set up similar makeshift arrangements.

PASTING TABLES

A flat surface is needed to lay the paper on while it is being pasted. It is best to use a proper pasting table. This is a lightweight folding table covered in hardboard or plywood on a softwood frame, and is usually about 1.8 m (6 ft) long and just wider than a standard roll of wall covering. If you cannot buy, borrow or hire a pasting table, one can be improvised by cutting a standard sheet of plywood or chipboard (particle board) down to the same width and supporting it on trestles or sawhorses.

SEAM ROLLERS

For smooth wall coverings, a tool called a seam roller can be used to make sure that the seams are well bonded to the wall. Do not use a seam roller on textured or embossed wall coverings, though, as it will flatten the embossing.

Displayed on a fold-up pasting table are a soaking trough (1), rubber gloves (2), sponge (3), pencil (4), sharp utility knife (5), paperhangers' scissors (6), plumb bob and line (7), retractable steel tape measure (8), steel straightedge (9), paste bucket (10), pasting brush (11), packet of ready-mixed paste (12), seam roller (13) and paperhanging brush (14). A spirit level (15) can do double duty in checking verticals and as a straightedge.

PREPARING FOR PAPERHANGING

Unrestricted access is a must for paperhanging. If working on just the walls, move all the furniture to the centre of the room and cover it with dust sheets (drop cloths). When tackling the ceiling too, it is best to remove all the furniture completely if there is space to store it elsewhere in the house; otherwise group it at one end of the room so that most of the ceiling can be done, and then move it to the other end to complete the job.

Next, take down curtains and blinds (drapes and shades) and remove wall-mounted or ceiling-mounted tracks. Turn off the electricity supply at the mains, then disconnect and remove wall or ceiling light fittings as necessary, covering the bare wire ends thoroughly with insulating tape before restoring the power supply to the rest of the house. In the USA, ceiling roses, wall switch plates and socket outlets can be unscrewed and removed without

disconnecting the wall receptacles or switches. Isolate, drain, disconnect and remove radiators, and unscrew their wall brackets. Call in a professional electrician or plumber for these jobs if unsure of how to do them safely.

Lift down pictures, and remove other wall-mounted fittings such as shelves and display units. To make it easy to relocate the screw holes afterwards, push a matchstick (wooden match) into each one (see Tip).

CHOOSING THE STARTING POINT

ABOVE Start paperhanging at the centre of a chimney breast (fireplace projection) if the wall covering has a large, dominant pattern. Otherwise start next to the door so the inevitable pattern break can be disguised above it.

RIGHT Work outwards from the centre of a dormer window so the design is centred on the window recess.

ESTIMATING WALL COVERINGS (WALLS)

Height	Distance around room																		
	9m 30ft	10m 33ft	12m 40ft	13m 42ft	14m 46ft	15m 50ft	16m 52ft	17m 56ft	19m 62ft	20m 66ft	21m 69ft	22m 72ft	23m 75ft	25m 82ft	26m 85ft	27m 88ft	28m 92ft	30m 98ft
2.15–2.30 m / 7–7½ ft	4	5	5	6	6	7	7	8	8	9	9	10	10	11	12	12	13	13
2.30–2.45 m / 7½–8 ft	5	5	6	6	7	7	8	8	9	9	10	10	11	11	12	13	13	14
2.45–2.60 m / 8–8½ ft	5	5	6	7	7	8	9	9	10	10	11	12	12	13	14	14	15	15
2.60–2.75 m / 8½–9 ft	5	5	6	7	7	8	9	9	10	10	11	12	12	13	14	14	15	15
2.75–2.90 m / 9–9½ ft	6	6	7	7	8	9	9	10	10	11	12	12	13	14	14	15	15	16
2.90–3.05 m / 9½–10 ft	6	6	7	8	8	9	10	10	11	12	12	13	14	14	15	16	16	17
3.05–3.20 m / 10–10½ ft	6	7	8	8	9	10	10	11	12	13	13	14	15	16	16	17	18	19

Numbers are based on a standard roll size of 10.05 m (33 ft) long and 520 mm (20½ in) wide. The measurement around the room includes all windows and doorway.

If the walls and ceiling are at present painted, they need washing down to remove dirt, grease, smoke stains and the like. If they are decorated with another wall covering, this will have to be removed and any defects in the surface put right. Finally, they need sizing – treating with a diluted coat of wallpaper adhesive to even out the porosity of the surface and to help to improve the 'slip' of the pasted wall covering during hanging.

Measuring up

The next job is to estimate how many rolls of wall covering will be needed to decorate the room. If using a material that comes in standard-sized rolls, simply measure the room dimensions and refer to the charts given here for the number of rolls needed to cover the walls and ceiling. They allow for a typical door and window area; fewer rolls are needed for a room with large picture windows or wide door openings. If using a paper-backed cloth covering which comes in a nonstandard width, measure up each wall, and ask the supplier to estimate what length of material you will need; such materials

are too expensive to waste. Wall coverings in the USA vary in width and length but are usually available in rolls sized to cover a specified area, allowing for trimming.

Buying wall coverings

Wall coverings are made in batches, with a number printed on the label, and it is important to check that there are

sufficient rolls with the same batch number; colours may not match exactly between batches.

When hanging a wall covering with a particularly large pattern repeat, wastage is often unusually high and it may be wise to purchase one or two extra rolls, over and above the numbers given in the charts. Most suppliers will take back unopened rolls.

ESTIMATING WALL COVERINGS (CEILINGS)

Distance around room		No of
m	ft	rolls
10	33	2
11	36	2
12	40	2
13	42	3
14	46	3
15	50	4
16	52	4
17	56	4
18	59	5
19	62	5
20	66	5
21	69	6
22	72	7
23	75	7

TIP

Insert a matchstick (wooden match) in each hole left when unscrewing wall-mounted fixtures and fittings that will be replaced later. It will burst through the wall covering as this is applied and make it easy to find the screw holes.

STRIPPING OLD WALL COVERINGS

In the days when ordinary printed wall coverings were all that were usually on sale, it was common practice to paper over existing wallpaper, often to the point where four or five successive layers would accumulate. This is no longer considered acceptable (and will not work at all over today's washable and vinyl wall coverings), and it is always best to strip all old coverings before hanging new ones. Even if the old material looks sound, hanging a newly-pasted wall covering over it may cause it to lift from the wall, creating ugly bubbles that are impossible to disguise. This also applies to the backing paper that is left on the wall after dry-stripping a vinyl wall covering; there is no guarantee that it is perfectly bonded to the wall, and so hanging another wall covering over it could give very poor results.

Once the room is cleared and dust sheets (drop cloths) are spread over the floor and any remaining furniture, the next step is to identify what type of wall covering is to be removed. An ordinary printed paper will absorb water splashed on it immediately; other types will not. To tell washables from vinyls, pick and lift a corner and try to strip the wall covering dry. The printed plastic layer of a vinyl wall covering will peel off dry, but the surface of a washable paper will not come off in the same way unless it is a duplex paper made in two layers. With paper-backed fabric wall coverings, it is often possible to peel the fabric away from its paper backing; try it before turning to other more complicated methods of removal.

1 To strip printed wallpapers, wet the surface with a sponge or a garden spray gun. Wait for the water to penetrate, and repeat if necessary.

2 Using a stiff wallpaper scraper – not a filling knife (putty knife) – start scraping the old paper from the wall at a seam. Wet it again while working if necessary.

3 Turn off the power before stripping around switches and other fittings, then loosen the faceplate screws to strip the wallpaper behind them.

4 After removing the bulk of the old wallpaper, go back over the wall surface and remove any remaining 'nibs' of paper with sponge/spray gun and scraper.

5 To strip a washable wallpaper, start by scoring the plastic coating with a serrated scraper or toothed roller, then soak and scrape as before.

6 For quicker results, use a steam stripper to remove washable papers. Press the steaming plate to the next area while stripping the area just steamed.

STRIPPING VINYLS

1 Strip vinyl wall coverings by lifting a corner to separate the vinyl layer from the paper backing. Strip it off by pulling it away from the wall surface.

2 Always soak and remove the plain backing paper left on the wall after stripping a vinyl. It may well not be a sound lining for a new wall covering.

PREPARING SURFACES FOR COVERING

Once the previous wall and ceiling decorations have been removed the next task is to restore any defects in the surfaces to be covered, and then to prepare them so that they present the perfect substrate for successful paperhanging.

The first step is to put down some heavy-duty plastic sheeting on the floor to catch splashes, and then to wash down the bare wall and ceiling surfaces thoroughly with strong household detergent or sugar soap (all-purpose cleaner), working from the bottom up on walls, and then to rinse them off with clean water, working this time from top to bottom on walls. Turn off the electricity supply first in case water gets into light switches and socket outlets (receptacles). Leave the surfaces to dry out thoroughly.

Next, repair defects such as cracks, holes and other surface damage which may have been concealed by the previous decorations, or even caused by their removal.

Finally, treat the wall and ceiling surfaces with a coat of size or diluted wallpaper paste, and leave this to dry before starting paperhanging. Size seals porous plaster, providing a surface with even absorption, and also makes it easier to slide the pasted lengths of wall covering into position on the wall.

PREPARING WALLS AND CEILINGS

1 Wash wall surfaces down with sugar soap (all-purpose cleaner) or detergent, working from the bottom up, then rinse them with clean water, working from the top down.

2 Wash ceilings with a floor mop or squeegee, after disconnecting and removing light fittings. Again, rinse off with clean water.

3 Fill cracks, holes and other defects in the wall and ceiling surfaces as appropriate, leave the filler to harden and then sand the repair down flush.

4 Apply a coat of size or diluted wallpaper paste to wall and ceiling surfaces that are to be papered, and leave them to dry before starting paperhanging.

CROSS-LINING

If the wall surface is in poor condition, has been previously decorated with gloss paint or is being decorated with a thin fabric wall covering, it is best to hang lining (liner) paper first. This is usually hung horizontally rather than vertically, with butt joints between lengths and with ends and edges trimmed just short of adjacent ceiling and wall surfaces. Use the same type of paste for the lining paper as for the subsequent wall covering.

MEASURING AND CUTTING TO LENGTH

1 For quick and easy calculations, mark the whole length of the pasting table at 300 mm (12 in) intervals with a pencil and metal straightedge.

2 Measure the length of wall covering needed for the drop, including trim allowances, and mark this on the paper. Cut the first piece to length.

PASTING WALL COVERINGS

1 Face the light to make it easy to spot any unpasted areas – they look dull, not shiny. Apply a generous band of paste down the centre of the length.

2 Align one edge of the wall covering with the edge of the pasting table, then brush the paste out towards that edge from the centre band.

3 Draw the length across to the other edge of the table, and apply paste out to that edge too. Check that there are no dry or thinly pasted areas.

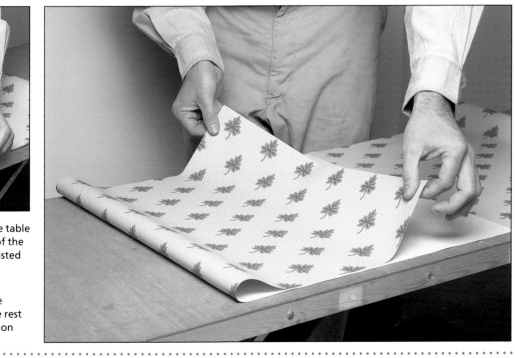

4 Continue pasting until the end of the table is reached. Then lift the pasted end of the wall covering and fold it over on itself, pasted side to pasted side.

5 Slide the paper along the table so the folded section hangs down. Paste the rest of the length and fold the other end over on itself as before.

PAPERHANGING

HANGING THE FIRST LENGTHS

The first length of wall covering must be hung correctly if the decoration of the rest of the room is to go according to plan. Therefore the first thing to do is to decide on exactly where this is to be hung. The usual starting point is close to the door, just less than the wall covering's width away from the frame, so that the inevitable pattern discontinuity that will occur on returning to the starting point can be concealed on the short join above the door. If using a wall covering with a large design motif in a room which has a chimney breast (fireplace projection) it is preferable to start paperhanging on the chimney breast itself so that the design can be centred on it. When papering only part of a room, the starting point should be just less than the width of the wall covering from one corner of the room, to allow the edge of the covering to be trimmed accurately into the corner angle.

Next, use a roll of wall covering as a yardstick and mark off successive widths round the room walls with a pencil to check that there will not be any joins on external corners such as the sides of window reveals. If these occur, move the starting point along by about 50 mm (2 in) and recheck the join positions all round.

Finally, mark a true vertical line on the wall at the chosen starting point, using a pencil and a plumb bob and line. Failure to do this could result in the pattern running seriously out of true as successive lengths are hung.

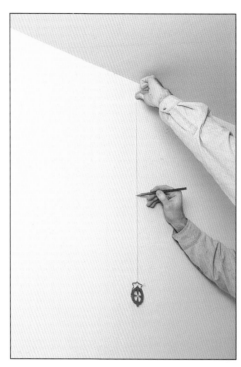

1 At the chosen starting point, use a plumb bob and line to mark a vertical line on the wall surface. Join up the pencil marks with a straightedge.

2 Fetch the first length of pasted wall covering after leaving it to soak for the time recommended on the label. Carry it draped over the arm.

6 Peel the end of the length away from the wall so the excess can be trimmed with scissors. Brush the end back into place. Repeat at the bottom.

3 Unfold the upper flap and press the top edge of the length against the wall. Slide it across the wall until the edge lines up with the marked line.

4 Use a paperhanging brush (or a sponge for washables and vinyls) to smooth the wall covering into place. Work from the middle out towards the edges.

5 Use a pencil or the curved back of paperhanging scissors blades to mark the trimming line at ceiling level. Do the same at floor level.

7 Hang the next drop with the lengths exactly edge to edge. Brush the wall covering into the wall/ceiling angle and into the internal angle.

8 On flat wall coverings, run a seam roller down the join to ensure that it sticks securely. Never use a seam roller on embossed or relief wall coverings.

TIP

If a seam refuses to lie flat because it was inadequately pasted and has begun to dry out, brush a little extra paste underneath it and roll it again.

PAPERHANGING AROUND CORNERS

In a perfect world, rooms would have corners that were truly square and truly vertical, and it would be possible to hang wall covering all around the room in a continuous operation, simply turning the lengths that ran into the room corners straight onto the adjoining walls. In reality, corners are seldom square or true, and if the covering was hung in this way, lengths would be vertical on the first wall but could be running well off the vertical by the time they returned to the starting point. The effect can be visually disastrous, with vertical pattern elements clearly out of alignment at corners and horizontal pattern features sloping relative to the ceiling or skirting (baseboard).

The way to avoid these problems is to complete each wall with a cut-down strip that only just turns onto the next wall, to conceal the join in the corner angle. Then hang the remainder of the strip with its machine-cut edge against a newly drawn vertical line on the second wall, so that its other edge can be trimmed to follow the internal angle precisely. Any slight pattern discontinuity that results will not be noticeable except to the closest scrutiny, and the remaining lengths on the second wall will be hung truly vertically. A similar process is used when paperhanging around external corners, as at window reveals and on chimney breasts (fireplace projections).

PAPERING INTERNAL CORNERS

1 Hang the last full length before the corner of the room, then measure the distance to the corner from the edge of the length and add about 12 mm (½ in).

2 Use a pencil and straightedge to mark a strip of the required width, measured from the relevant edge (here, the left one), and cut it from the length.

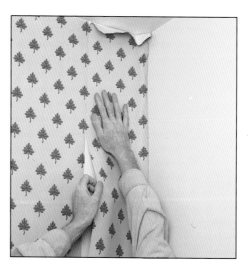

3 Paste the strip and hang it in the usual way, allowing the hand-cut edge to lap onto the adjoining wall. Trim the top and bottom edges as usual.

4 Brush the tongue into the internal angle. If it will not lie flat because the corner is out of true, make small release cuts in the edge and brush it flat.

5 Measure the width of the remaining strip, subtract 12 mm (½ in) and mark a fresh vertical line on the adjoining wall at this distance from the corner.

6 Hang the strip to the marked line, brushing the wall covering into the angle so it just turns onto the surface of the first wall.

7 Use the back of the scissors blades to mark the line of the corner on the wall covering, then cut along the line and smooth the cut edge back into the angle. Use special overlap adhesive when using washables and vinyls on all lap joints.

PAPERING EXTERNAL CORNERS

1 Plan the starting point so that lengths turn external corners by about 25 mm (1 in). Brush the paper onto the next wall, making small cuts so it lies flat.

2 Carefully tear off a narrow strip of the wall covering along the turned edge to leave a 'feathered' edge that will not show through the next length.

3 Mark a vertical line on the next wall surface at a distance from the corner equal to the width of the wall covering plus about 6 mm (¼ in).

4 Hang the next full length to the marked line, with its other edge overlapping the feathered edge of the strip turned from the previous wall.

5 Brush this length into position, trim it at top and bottom as before, and run a seam roller down the overlap (not on embossed or textured wall coverings). Again, use a special overlap adhesive with washables and vinyls.

Paperhanging on flat, uninterrupted walls is quite straightforward, calling only for the basic positioning and trimming techniques. Turning corners is only slightly more difficult. The trouble is that rooms also contain doors, windows and wall-mounted fittings and fixtures such as light switches and socket outlets (receptacles). Paperhanging around these obstacles can be tricky, but there are procedures for dealing with them.

Doors and window frames fitted flush with the internal wall surface present few problems; all that is necessary is to trim the wall covering so it finishes flush with the edge of the architrave (trim) or casing. Where the window or door is recessed, some careful patching-in of extra pieces is needed to cover all the surfaces of the reveal. It is also important to select the starting point to avoid joins between lengths falling on the external corners of such reveals; always check this point before beginning paperhanging, and adjust the starting point by about 50 mm (2 in) if it will occur.

Paperhanging round electrical fittings (fixtures) is not so difficult. The idea is to make diagonal cuts over the faceplate, cut away most of the resulting triangular tongues and tuck what is left behind the loosened faceplate. Always turn the power supply to the accessory off first. Do not do this with vinyl foils, which can conduct electricity; instead, simply trim the covering flush with the edges of the accessory faceplate. In the USA wall plates and socket outlets can be removed separately without disconnecting the wall receptacles or switches, which makes the task much simpler.

PAPERING AROUND FLUSH DOORS AND WINDOWS

1 On reaching a flush door or window frame, hang the previous length as normal. Then hang the next length to overlap the door or window frame.

2 Cut away the unwanted wall covering to within about 25 mm (1 in) of the edge of the architrave (trim) or window casing, and discard the waste strip.

3 Press the covering against the frame so that its corner is visible, and make a diagonal cut from the waste edge of the paper to the mark.

4 Use the paperhanging brush to press the tongues of paper well into the angles between the wall and the door architrave or window casing.

5 Peel back the tongues carefully and cut along the marked lines with paperhanging scissors. Then brush the trimmed edges back into position.

PAPERING AROUND RECESSED DOORS AND WINDOWS

1 On reaching a recessed door or window frame, hang the previous length as normal. Then hang the next length, allowing it to overlap the recess.

2 Make a horizontal cut into the overlapping edge level with the underside of the reveal to allow the central portion of the length to cover the side wall.

PAPERING AROUND ELECTRICAL FITTINGS (FIXTURES)

Make diagonal cuts towards the corners, trim off the triangles and tuck the edges behind the loosened faceplate. The power must be turned off first.

3 On recessed windows, make a similar cut lower down the length, level with the top surface of the window sill. Then trim it to fit round the end of the sill.

4 Cut a patch to fit on the underside of the reveal, big enough to turn onto adjoining wall and frame surfaces. Press it well into the internal angles.

5 Tear along the edges of the patch that will be covered when the piece above the reveal and the tongue covering its side wall are brushed into place.

6 Trim the edges of the patch and tongue to meet the frame neatly. Then hang full widths when the other side of the reveal is reached, and repeat steps 1–6.

PAPERING STAIRWELLS

Paperhanging in stairwells is no different in principle from work in any other room. However, the job is made more difficult by the need to handle longer lengths of wall covering, and also because access to the higher reaches of the stairwell walls can be awkward. It is a job that requires careful planning, and is best tackled with the assistance of a second person.

First of all, work out the starting point. It is best to hang the longest drop – the one that reaches from landing ceiling to hall floor – first of all. Mark its position and check that other joins will not fall awkwardly round the rest of the stairwell, especially if it has a window opening onto it. Adjust the starting point if necessary.

The next thing to do is to work out how to gain access to the various wall surfaces involved without obstructing passage up and down the stairwell or blocking off the walls themselves. On a straight flight it may be possible to use components from a hired slot-together scaffold tower to make a suitable working platform. On flights with quarter or half-landings it will probably be necessary to tailor-make an assembly of ladder sections, stepladders, homemade supports and scaffold boards; two typical arrangements are shown in the illustrations. Nail scrap wood to stair treads to locate ladder feet securely, and lock scaffold boards together by drilling holes through them where they overlap and dropping a bolt through the holes (no need for a nut). Note that ladders or steps shown resting against wall surfaces will have to be repositioned as the work progresses.

ACCESS EQUIPMENT FOR STAIRWELLS

Use a selection of ladders, steps, scaffold boards and homemade supports to construct a platform that allows access to all the wall surfaces being decorated without obstructing the stairs themselves.

STARTING POINT

Aim to start work by hanging the longest drop first. Then work along the stairwell walls in sequence, turning corners and tackling obstacles as for other rooms.

1 Fold up long lengths of wall covering concertina-fashion with the top end of the length uppermost, and carry them to the stairs supported over the arm.

2 Get a helper to support the folds of wall covering while positioning the top end of the length on the stairwell wall against a vertical line.

3 When measuring lengths that will meet a dado (chair) rail or skirting (baseboard) at an angle, remember to measure the longer edge of the length.

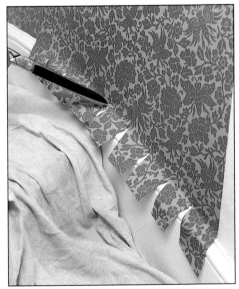

4 Where the bottom edge of the length meets a shaped skirting, make small release cuts in the edge and trim it to follow the curve.

PAPERING AROUND OBSTACLES

Where the end of a handrail fits flush with the wall, cut the lower part of the length into two strips so their edges can be trimmed around the rail and joined edge to edge beneath it. Use a similar technique to fit the wall covering around a flush newel post.

PAPERING CEILINGS

Many people regard the papering of ceilings with horror. In reality they are easier to deal with than walls because they are flat, do not have any awkward angles (except in rooms with sloping ceilings and dormer windows), and have few obstacles attached to them apart from the occasional light fitting (fixture), which can in any case usually be removed quite easily.

The only thing that takes getting used to when papering ceilings is working on an upside-down surface, but the basic technique is no different from working on walls. The wall covering is simply positioned, brushed into place and then trimmed where it meets adjoining surfaces.

The most important thing to plan carefully is access equipment that will allow a complete length to be hung across the room. Nothing is more dangerous than attempting to step from chair to chair; proper access is a must. The best solution is to use scaffold boards or lengths of staging, supported by stepladders, trestles or homemade supports to create a flat, level walkway spanning the room from wall to wall at a height that allows the ceiling to be reached comfortably. It will take only a few seconds to reposition after hanging each length, ready for the next.

This is also a job where an additional pair of hands will be a big help, at least before gaining the knack of supporting a concertina of pasted wall covering with one hand while brushing it into position with the other. This can be done only with practice.

The first length should be hung to a guideline on the ceiling. The best way of marking this is with a chalked line, held against the ceiling at both ends and snapped against it. Use red chalk for a white ceiling.

1 Paste the wall covering in the usual way, but fold it up concertina-fashion with the starting end of the length folded over on itself. Lining (liner) paper has been used here.

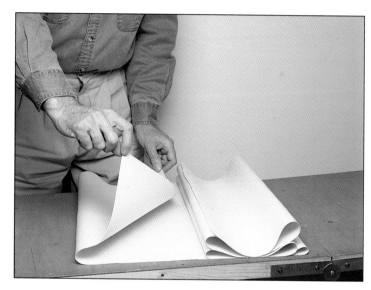

ACCESS EQUIPMENT FOR CEILINGS

Set up an access platform across the room, using scaffold boards supported on staging or stepladders, to create a walkway at a height that allows the ceiling to be comfortably reached.

2 Hang the first length to a chalked line just less than the width of the wall covering from the side wall. Support the folds on a spare roll of wall covering.

PAPERING ARCHES

The shape of an arch makes it impossible to get a pattern match along the curved join. It is best to choose a wall covering with a small design motif and a random pattern, to use different but complementary designs for the face walls and the arch surface, or to use lining (liner) paper inside the arch and paint it a plain colour.

To paper an arched recess, cover the face and back walls first, turning cut tongues of wall covering onto the arched surface. Then cover the arch surface as described below.

3 Trim the overlaps at the ends and along the side wall. Then hang the second length in the same way, butted up against the edge of the first length.

4 On meeting a pendant light fitting (fixture) pierce the wall covering over its centre and make a series of radial cuts outwards from the pierced point.

To paper a through archway, hang the wall covering on the two face walls and trim out the waste to leave an overlap of about 25 mm (1 in) all around. Make cuts in the edge so that the tongues can be turned onto the arch surface. Then cut a strip of wall covering a fraction narrower than the width of the arch surface and long enough to cover it in one piece, and brush this into place. Work from the bottom of one side upwards to the top of the arch, and then down the other side. Always use special overlap adhesive with washables and vinyls.

5 With the power turned off at the mains, unscrew the cover and trim the tongues off flush with the base of the fitting. Replace the cover to conceal the cut ends.

6 Where the ceiling runs into an alcove, cut the wall covering in line with the side wall of the recess and brush it into place. Trim off the waste section.

OTHER PAPERHANGING TECHNIQUES

Apart from the traditional method of pasting the wall covering on a pasting table and then hanging it on the wall, two other techniques may sometimes be needed. The first is hanging ready-pasted wall coverings, which are growing in popularity, while the second is hanging speciality wall coverings.

Hanging ready-pasted wall coverings could not be easier. The back of the wall covering – usually a washable or vinyl type, for obvious reasons – is coated during manufacture with an even layer of dried paste. To activate this, simply cut the length that is needed, roll it up with the top of the length on the outside of the roll, and immerse it in water. Special soaking troughs are sold by most wall covering suppliers, and are intended to be placed next to the skirting (baseboard) beneath the point where the length is to be hung. The trough is filled with cold (not hot) water, the length is immersed and drawn upwards onto the wall so that excess water drains back into the trough. It is then hung and trimmed in the usual way.

Many speciality wall coverings are designed to be hung by pasting the wall, not the wall covering. Some also have untrimmed edges, which need to be cut after overlapping adjoining lengths. The technique is, however, quite straightforward.

HANGING READY-PASTED WALL COVERINGS

1 Place the trough next to the wall, fill it with cold water and immerse the rolled-up length in it, top end outermost, for the recommended time.

2 At the end of the recommended soaking time, grasp the top end of the length and draw it upwards so that the excess water runs off it back into the trough.

3 Slide the top of the length into position on the wall, aligning it with a marked line or butting it up against its neighbour. Do not step in the trough.

4 Use a sponge rather than a paperhanging brush to smooth the length into place on the wall. This helps to absorb excess water from the surface.

1 Cut the wall covering to the length required, including a trim allowance, and roll it up face inwards around a broom handle or similar object.

2 Apply the recommended paste (usually a thick ready-mixed type) to the wall, and then unroll the wall covering onto the wet paste against a marked line.

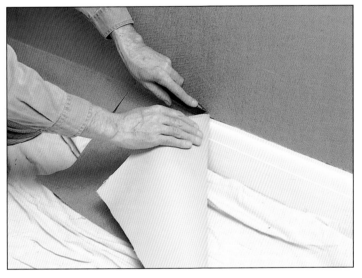

3 Run a clean, dry paint roller backwards and forwards over the surface of the wall covering to bond it firmly to the wall.

4 Use a sharp utility knife – and a straightedge if needed – to trim the wall covering where it meets the ceiling and the skirting (baseboard).

5 To create neat joins, overlap adjoining lengths slightly and then cut through both layers with a sharp utility knife run along a straightedge.

6 Peel away the two waste strips and smooth the cut edges neatly back into place. Run a seam roller along the seam to ensure a good bond.

PUTTING UP FRIEZES AND BORDERS

Friezes and borders are narrow strips of printed paper or vinyl wall covering sold in rolls, and often come in colours and designs that complement wall coverings and fabrics manufactured by the same firm. A frieze is usually applied as a horizontal band running around the room, and can be positioned at ceiling level or next to a picture rail or dado (chair) rail. Borders, on the other hand, are used either to frame features of the room such as a door or window opening, or to create decorative panels on wall or ceiling surfaces – perhaps to frame a group of pictures, for example. They come in a range of widths.

Friezes and borders are available in plain and self-adhesive versions. The former is pasted in the same way as an ordinary wall covering, so this type is ideal for use on walls that have been painted or decorated with a plain printed wallpaper. If a border or frieze is to go over a washable or vinyl wall covering, use a special overlap adhesive or choose a self-adhesive type since ordinary wallpaper paste will not stick to the surface of the covering. Simply cut these to length, then peel off the backing paper bit by bit while positioning the length on the wall.

TIP

To gauge the effect a frieze or border will have, and to decide on the best position for it, stick lengths to the wall surface with masking tape before fixing them up permanently.

APPLYING A FRIEZE

1 Decide on the precise position of the frieze or border, then measure the distance from a nearby feature such as a ceiling or door frame.

2 Use a spirit level and pencil to draw true horizontal and vertical guidelines on the wall or ceiling surface at the marked position.

3 Cut the frieze or border to length and carefully apply paste to the length. Fold it up concertina fashion while working along it.

4 Offer the free end of the concertina up to the marked line and brush it into place. It will help to have an assistant when hanging long lengths.

5 Join successive lengths end to end when starting a new roll. If the pattern does not match, overlap the ends so it does and cut through both layers.

6 Finally, check that all horizontal edges and vertical joints are well bonded to the wall by running over them with a seam roller. Remove excess paste.

APPLYING A BORDER

1 Put up the individual lengths of a border in the same way as a frieze. To form corners, overlap the lengths at right angles and cut through both layers at 45°.

2 Peel away the two waste sections and press the neatly mitred ends back into place. Adjust their positions if necessary to get a perfect joint.

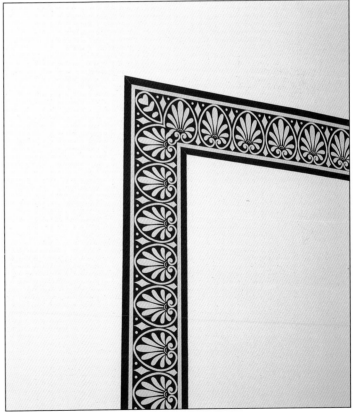

3 The finished corner joint shows how accurate alignment and careful cutting result in a neat joint with the pattern meeting along the mitred cuts.

REPAIRING WALL COVERINGS

It is a simple matter to repair minor damage to painted walls and ceilings and then to cover it up with a fresh coat of paint. With wall coverings, patching damage or curing paperhanging defects requires a different approach.

The commonest form of damage to a wall covering is an impact that leaves a jagged tear. If the torn part is still attached, brush some paste onto its rear face and press it back into place, rolling it flat with a seam roller.

If the torn part is missing it will be necessary to patch the damage. If there are some offcuts from the original papering job, cut a patch from them. If not, cut and dry-strip a patch from an out-of-sight area behind a piece of furniture to use for the repair. Tear around the edges of the patch, holding it face down, to create a thin 'feathered' edge, then paste it, place it over the damaged area and flatten it with a seam roller. If the paper is a thick two-layer duplex type, try to peel away the backing paper to reduce the thickness of the patch.

Two other common problems, blisters and lifting seams, are the result of inadequate pasting during paperhanging. It is a relatively simple task to slit blisters open and lift dry seams to apply a little fresh paste and stick the covering firmly back to the wall. With fragile printed or flocked wall coverings, take care not to get paste on the surface.

PATCHING DAMAGED WALLPAPER

1 Cut a repair patch from an offcut of the original wall covering, or strip one from behind a piece of furniture. Check that it will cover the damage and match the pattern.

CURING DRY BLISTERS

1 If a dry blister appears after wallpapering, use a sharp utility knife to make two cuts through it at right angles.

2 Peel back the triangular tongues formed and apply a little paste to the wall surface and to the back of the tongues. Leave to soak for a few minutes.

3 Press the triangles back into place and run a seam roller along the cuts to bond the paper firmly to the wall and leave an almost invisible repair.

3 BELOW Some two-layer duplex papers are too thick to use as a patch. Try to separate the backing paper at a corner of the patch and peel it off.

2 ABOVE Carefully tear along the edges of the patch to reduce its thickness and create a thin feathered edge. Check that no backing paper is visible.

4 BELOW Paste the back of the patch and place it over the damaged area, aligning the pattern carefully. Then 'iron' it into place with a seam roller.

STICKING DRY SEAMS

1 If a seam has failed to stick flat, lift it with a filling knife (putty knife) and use a slip of abrasive paper to sand off the dried paste behind it.

2 Use the filling knife to hold the edge of the wall covering away from the wall, and brush a little paste onto the back and the wall surface. Leave to soak.

3 Press the seam down flat with a seam roller, then use a sponge or damp cloth to remove any paste that has oozed onto the face of the wall covering.

INDEX

aerosol paints, 25
arches, papering, 57

bathrooms, 37
bedrooms, 10, 12
binders, 10
borders, paperhanging, 60-1
brushes, using, 22-3

ceilings
  painting, 26-7
  papering, 56-7
children's rooms, 11, 37
colour washing, 31
cross-lining, wall coverings, 46

doors, papering around, 52-3
dragging, 32
duplex papers, 36

equipment
  cleaning, 12
  painting, 14-15, 22-5
  paperhanging, 40-1

fabric wall coverings, 38
flock wall coverings, 38
foamed polythene, 38
foamed vinyl wall coverings, 37
friezes, paperhanging, 60-1

glazes, 28-9
graining, 32

hessian, 38

kitchens, 10, 37
knotting, 12

lining paper, 39

marbling, 33
matt finishes, 10
metal, paints for, 12

paint brushes
  cleaning, 12
  using, 22-3
paint pads, 24-5

paint rollers, 24
painting, 9-33
  preparing surfaces, 18-19, 29
  special effects, 28-33
  tools, 14-15, 22-5
  walls, 26-7
paints
  aerosol, 25
  coverage, 26
  estimating quantities, 26
  for wallpapers, 39
  stripping, 20-1
  texture, 26-7
  types of, 10-11
paperhanging, 35-63
  arches, 57
  around corners, 50-1
  around doors, 52-3
  around electrical fittings, 53
  around obstacles, 55
  around windows, 52-3
  blisters, 62
  borders, 60-1
  ceilings, 56-7
  cross-lining, 46
  estimating quantities, 43
  friezes, 60-1
  hanging, 48-9
  measuring lengths, 47
  pasting, 47
  patching, 62-3
  preparation, 42-7
  ready-pasted covering, 58
  seams, 49, 63
  speciality wall coverings, 59
  stairwells, 54-5
  stripping walls, 44-5
  tools, 40-1
  work sequence, 42
pasting, wall coverings, 47
pasting tables, 41
pigments, 10
preparing surfaces
  for painting, 18-19, 29
  for paperhanging, 43, 44-7
primers, 11, 12

rag-rolling, 30
relief wall coverings, 38-9
rollers, 24

sealers, 11
  special paint effects, 33
seam rollers, 41
self-undercoating paints, 12
shellac, 12
sponging, 30
stains
  painting over, 19
  wood, 12-13
stairwells, papering, 54-5
stencils, 29
stepladders, 26
stippling, 31
stripping
  paint, 20-1
  wall coverings, 44-5
surfaces
  preparing for painting, 18-19, 29
  preparing for paperhanging, 43, 44-7
switches, papering around, 53

texture paint, 26-7
textured wall coverings, 38
thixotropic paint, 11
tools
  painting, 14-15, 22-5
  paperhanging, 40-1
top coats, 12

undercoats, 11

varnishes, 12-13
  sealing paint effects, 33
vinyl foils, 37
vinyl wall coverings, 37, 38
  stripping, 45

wall coverings
  buying, 43
  estimating quantities, 43
  repairing, 62-3
  stripping, 44-5
  types, 36-9
  see also individual types of covering
  eg vinyl foils
washable wallpapers, 36
water-based paints, 9
windows, papering around, 52-3
wood, paints for, 12
wood stains, 12-13
woodchip paper, 38